BARRIER ISLAND BREACHES

JAMAICA BAY PAMPHLET LIBRARY 07

BARRIER ISLAND BREACHES

STRUCTURES OF COASTAL RESILIENCE
Jamaica Bay Team
Spitzer School of Architecture
The City College of New York

Catherine Seavitt Nordenson, editor
Associate Professor of Landscape Architecture

Kjirsten Alexander
Research Associate

Danae Alessi
Research Associate

Eli Sands
Research Assistant

JAMAICA BAY PAMPHLET LIBRARY
07 Barrier Island Breaches

ISBN 978-1-942900-07-8

COPYRIGHT

CONTACT

Catherine Seavitt Nordenson
cseavittnordenson@ccny.cuny.edu
www.structuresofcoastalresilience.org

SCR Jamaica Bay Team
The City College of New York
Spitzer School of Architecture
Program in Landscape Architecture, Room 2M24A
141 Convent Avenue New York, New York 10031

COVER

Shinnecock Inlet, 1999.
source: lishore.org and Stonybrook State University of New York

supported by

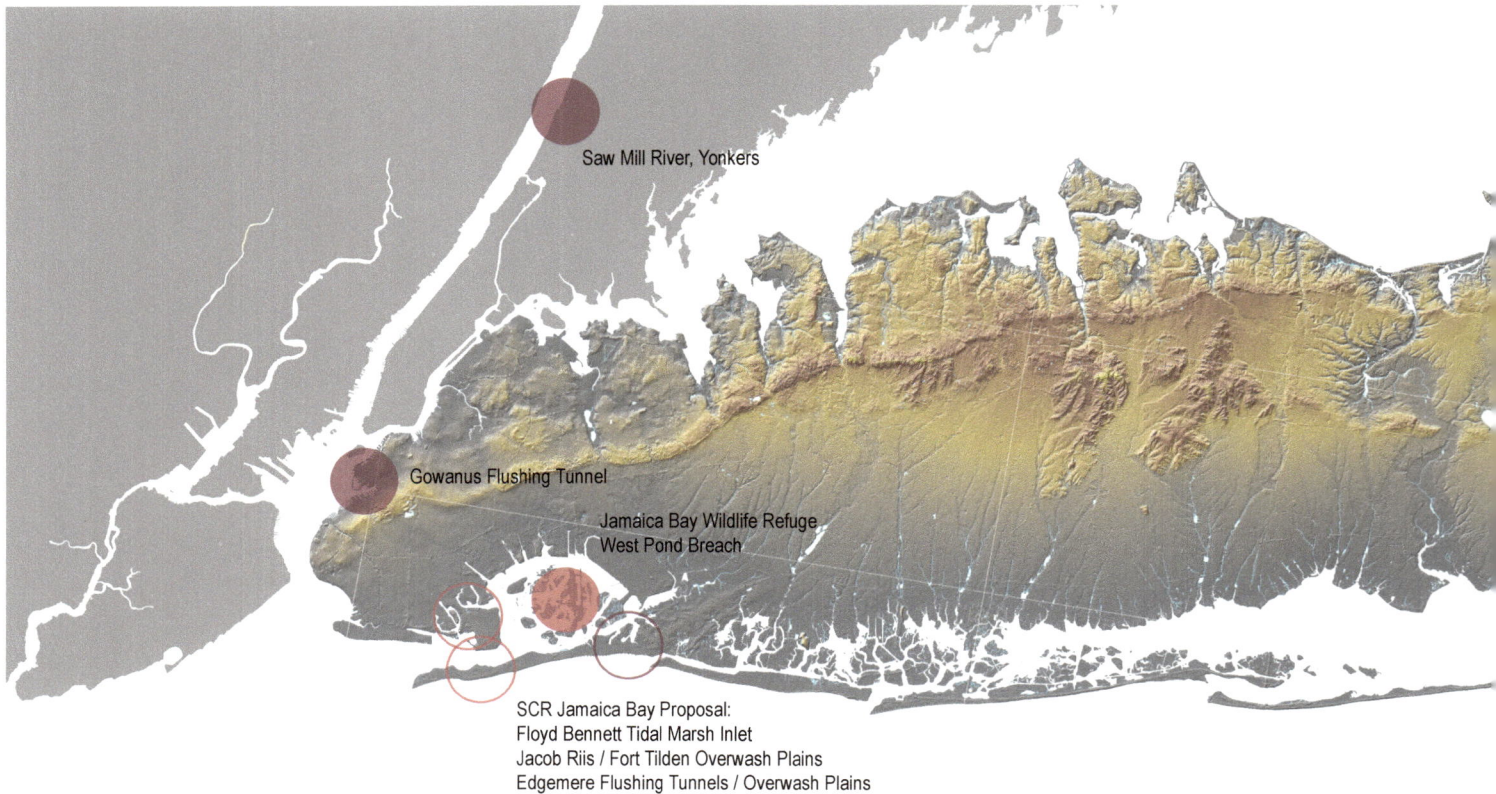

Saw Mill River, Yonkers

Gowanus Flushing Tunnel

Jamaica Bay Wildlife Refuge
West Pond Breach

SCR Jamaica Bay Proposal:
Floyd Bennett Tidal Marsh Inlet
Jacob Riis / Fort Tilden Overwash Plains
Edgemere Flushing Tunnels / Overwash Plains

Barrier island chains form a thin, sandy line parallel to the mainland coast. It is theorized that they formed after the last ice age when sea levels rose and sediment was carried to and deposited on the shallow coastal shelf. Wind, waves, and currents driving littoral drift, or sand migrating along the shore, continue to shape these islands. Behind them, shallow estuarine embayments form, unique ecosystems that provide valuable habitat due to their salinity, depths, shelter from wind and waves, and protection from many ocean predators.

At the southern shore of Long Island, a narrow, discontinuous line of islands is constantly shifting, with new inlets forming and old ones closing. Barrier islands, unless stabilized through human intervention, will typically "roll over" from the ocean towards the bay both in episodic storm events and through constant tidal processes, allowing sediment to migrate inwards. Incidents of breaching deliver sediment to the bay, supporting the marshes

within. A breach or overwash can also act as an outlet for flood waters and improve water quality through increased flushing.

According to the US Army Corps of Engineers (USACE), "A breach is a new opening in a narrow landmass such as a barrier spit or barrier island that allows water to flow between the water bodies on each side. (...) Breaches occur naturally or they can be purposefully dug or dredged, and a breach may have positive or negative consequences." (Kraus and Wamsley, 2003)

Breaching may occur by overtopping, either from the ocean in the event of a storm with high surge and large waves, or from the bay when water levels are raised due to heavy rainfall. Breaching may also occur due to seepage and liquefaction, when the porous substrate is infiltrated and turns to slurry, typically from the bay side. Breaching is most likely to occur where an area of lower elevation allows an entry point for water and then scour further erodes the channel.

base map source: USGS

Georgica Cove

Sagaponack Pond

Mecox Bay

Shinnecock Canal
Shinnecock Inlet

Moriches Inlet

Old Inlet, Fire Island

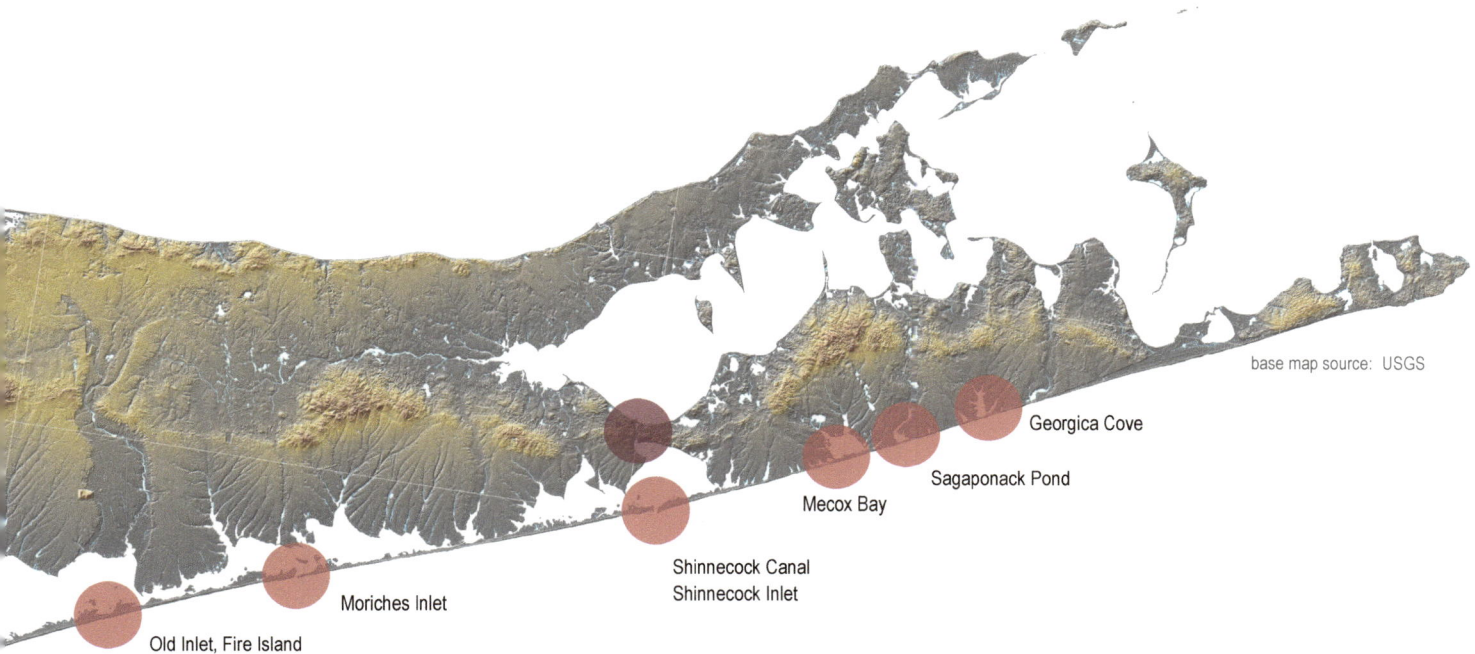

Many of the breaches along the barrier islands of Long Island are heavily managed for various purposes. The barrier islands form a protective buffer against wind and waves, and breaches or inlets through these islands are key to USACE's mission of maintaining access to the federal navigational channel known as the Intracoastal Waterway in the sheltered bays behind them.

Some breaches are mechanically opened for ecological and flood control reasons, such as Mecox Bay, Sagaponack Pond, and Georgica Cove. Other breaches such as Moriches Inlet and Shinnecock Inlet occurred in major storms and were stabilized with jetties and rock edges to maintain navigation channels.

With increasing urbanization, homes and infrastructure have been built on barrier islands, creating an expectation of stability and permanency. Despite the natural disturbances that continually shape these landforms, great efforts and resources are expended trying to stabilize them. However, given the expected increase in both the frequency and intensity of storms due to climate change, storm events and erosion will likely cause these barrier islands to transform.

sources

Coastal Barrier Island Breaching, Part 1: Overview of Breaching Processes, Nicholas C. Kraus, Ty V. Wamsley, for US Army Corps of Engineers, ERDC/CHL CHETN-IV-56, March 2003.

Coastal Barrier Island Breaching, Part 2: Mechanical Breaching and Breach Closure, Nicholas C. Kraus, Ty V. Wamsley, for US Army Corps of Engineers, ERDC/CHL CHETN-IV-65, August 2005.

Recommendations for a Barrier Island Breach Management Plan for Fire Island National Seashore, Including the Otis Pike High Dune Wilderness Area, Long Island, New York. National Park Service, US Department of the Interior, Northeast Region, Boston, MA. S. Jeffress Williams and Mary K. Foley, February 2007.

Old Inlet, Fire Island

The Fire Island National Seashore is a 20,000 acre unit of the National Park System including a 32-mile coastal barrier island, seven miles of which are designated a Federal Wilderness Area. The National Park Service Management Policy from 2006, Chapter 4.8.1 states that the Service must "allow natural geologic processes to proceed unimpeded... across a broad spectrum of space and time." The challenge is to "maintain natural coastal

November 2012
photo: National Park Service

processes to the greatest extent possible" while balancing environmental conservation and sustainability with the prevention of damage to development and loss of human life. The National Park Service does allow breach closure within the Fire Island National Seashore based on factors such as sediment, water, and nutrient exchange; increased tidal range; an economic cost-benefit analysis; and methods of artificial closure.

USACE s Breach Management Plan from 1996 states that in the event of a breach, "closure would be initiated within 72 hours of termination of a storm event... excluding the Federal Wilderness Area [which would be] monitored for indications of natural breach closure. If this does not occur, or if there is an increase in tidal ranges within the Great South Bay that can potentially flood developments...the breach would then be [mechanically] closed."

April 2013
photo: National Park Service

Old Inlet, Fire Island

In October of 2012, Hurricane Sandy opened a breach within the Otis Pike Fire Island High Dune Wilderness Area. Historically, breaches have occurred near this location and closed on their own. This breach has grown from 200 feet in November of 2012 to 2000 feet in September of 2013 and its shoreline, bathymetry, and tidal discharge are being monitored. As of August 2014, the National Park Service has not called for mechanical closure of the breach.

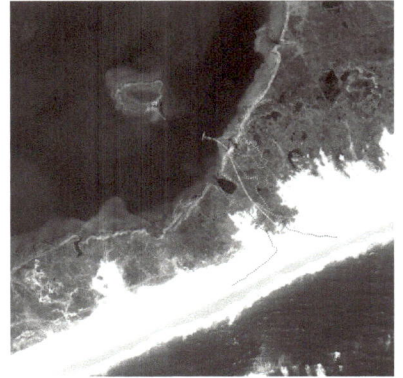

March 2012

February 2013

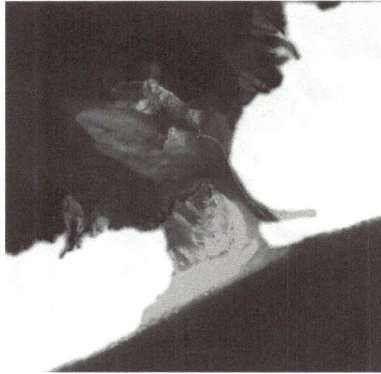

March 2013

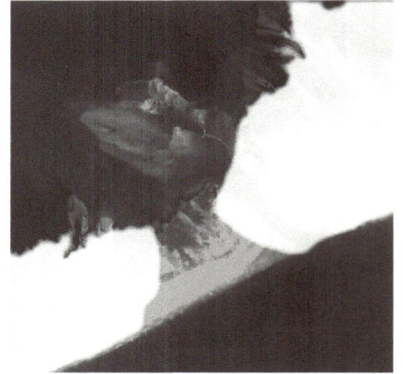

April 2013

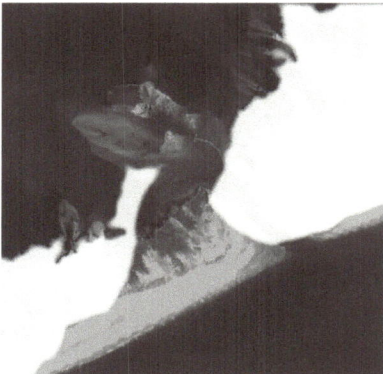

June 2013

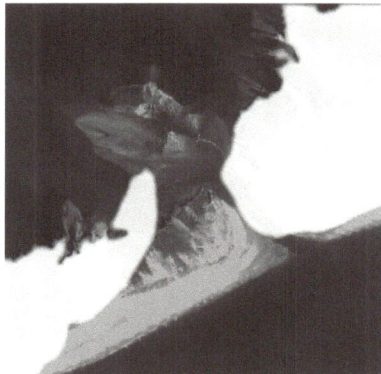

July 2013

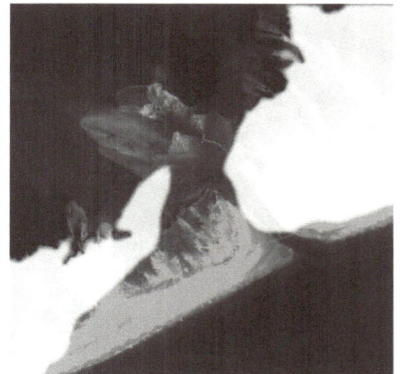

August 2013

November 2012

December 2012

January 2013

May 2013

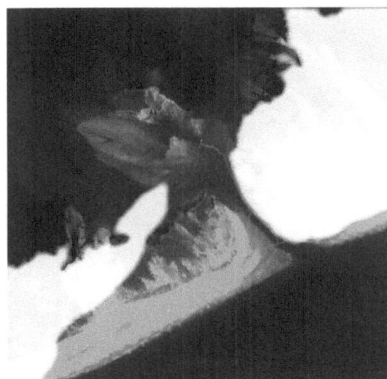

September 2013

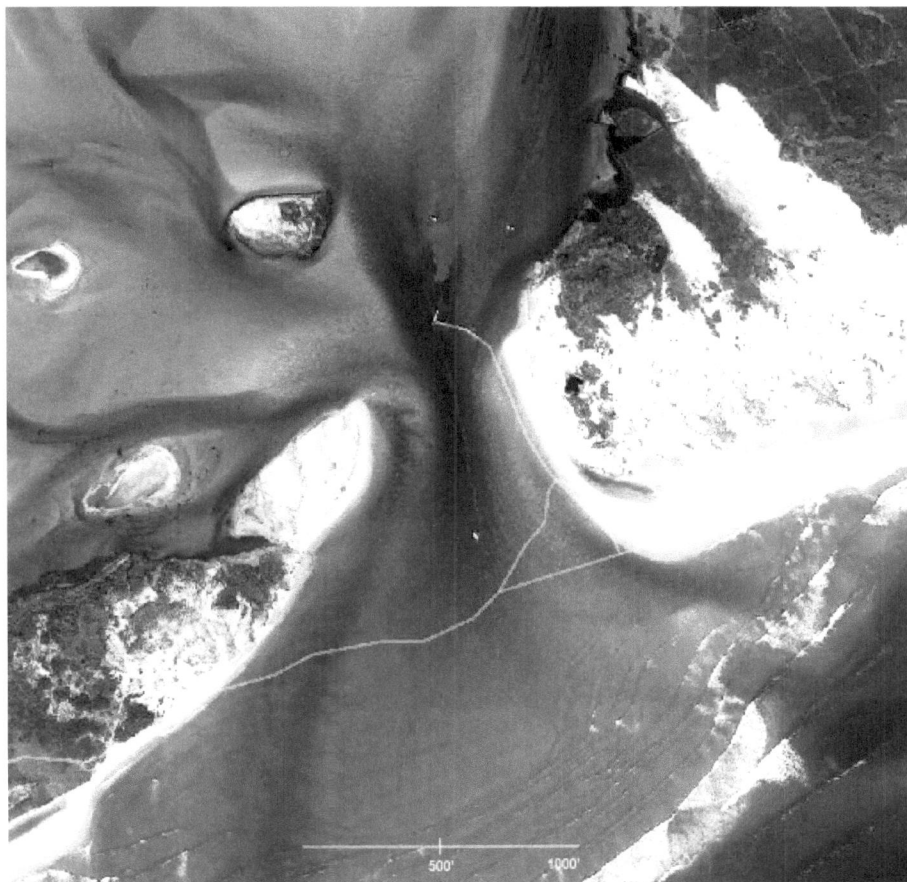

September 2013

Moriches Inlet

Moriches Inlet formed during the Nor'easter of 1931 and widened to 4000 feet with the Long Island Express Hurricane in 1938. This storm also created the Shinnecock Inlet to the east, which alleviated the pressures of erosion at Moriches Inlet and prevented it from growing vastly wider. In 1952 two rubble-mound groins were installed on each side of the inlet to make it permanently 700 feet wide. Today USACE maintains the inlet as a 10-foot deep, 200-foot wide, 0.8-mile long channel that provides access to the Long Island Intracoastal Waterway.

Moriches Inlet is at the far eastern edge of Fire Island and many argue that its groins intercept east-west longshore drift, resulting in sand starved beaches and dunes in the protected National Seashore to the west. Although longshore drift deposits sand along the eastern Moriches jetty, strong ebb currents eroded the bay side of the barrier island eash of the inlet which eventually breached in a storm in 1980. Due to concerns about increased flooding and impacts on shellfish habitat, within a year USACE closed the breach using 1.2 million cubic yards of fill, half of which was sourced from maintenance dredging nearby.

During Hurricane Sandy, 2012, a 350-foot wide breach opened through the sand bar at Cupsogue County Park, just east of Moriches inlet, which activated the Army Corps' Breach Contingency Plan. It was mechanically closed within a month using 200,000 cubic yards of sand at a cost of $6 million.

Moriches Inlet, looking east
photo: PhotoLenzOnline Aerial Photography

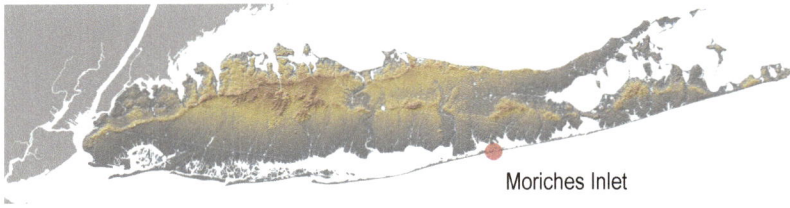

Moriches Inlet

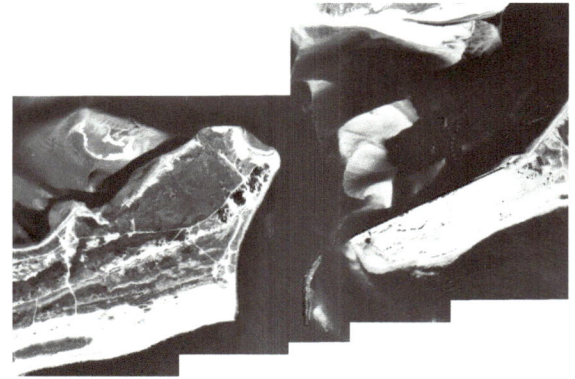

Moriches Inlet breach fill construction, December 1980
source: US Army Corps of Engineers

April 2004

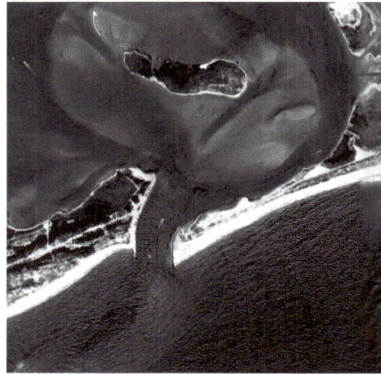

June 2005

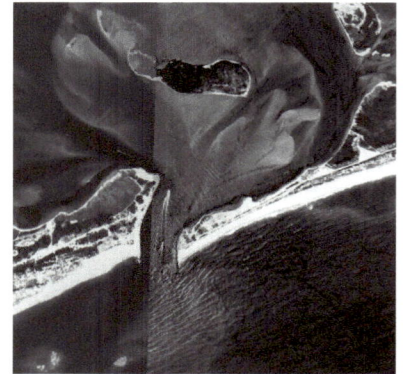

November 2006

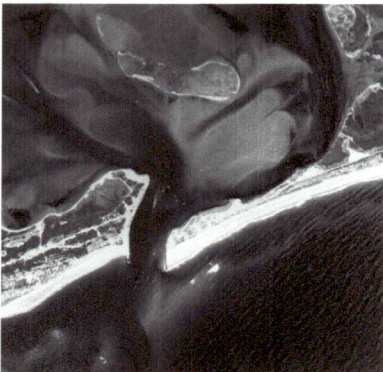

September 2009

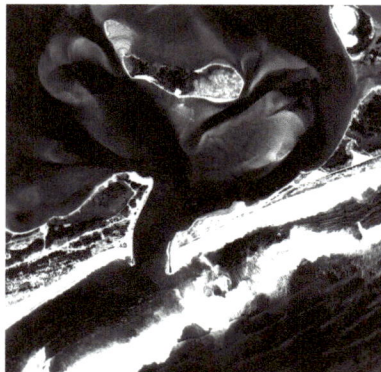

September 2010

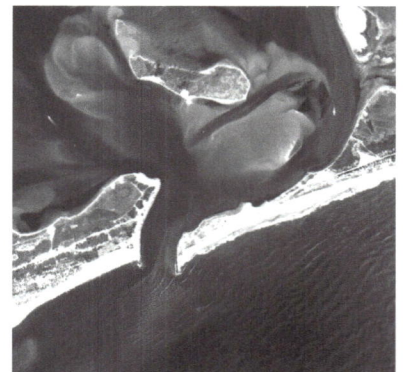

November 2011

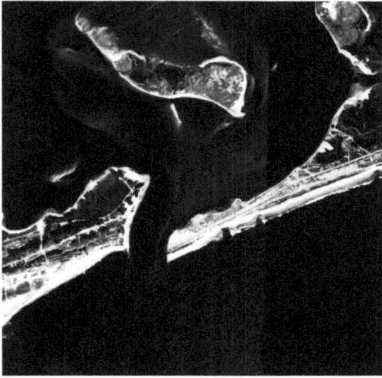

April 1994

April 2001

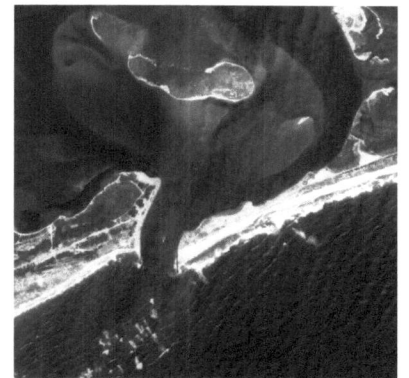

June 2003

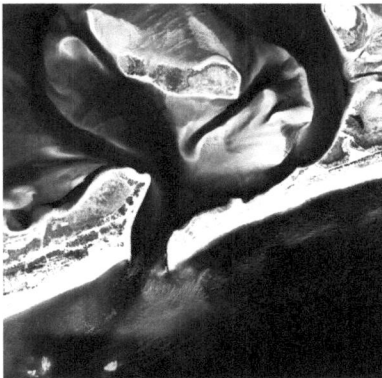

March 2007

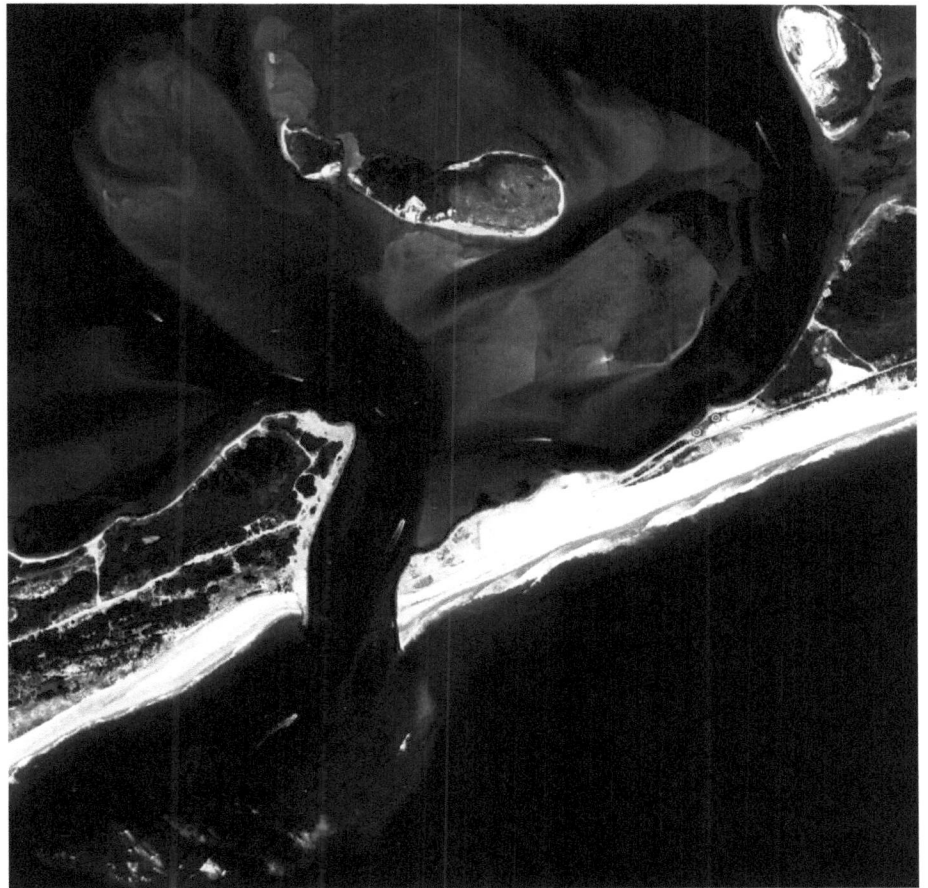

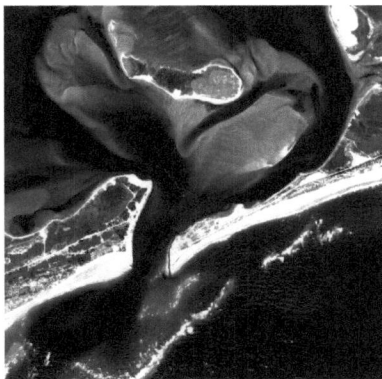

March 2012

September 2013

Shinnecock Inlet

Shinnecock Inlet was one of ten new breaches created in 1938 by the Long Island Express Hurricane, which had peak steady winds of 120 mph and peak storm surge of 16.75 feet above Mean Lower Low Water at Willets Point in New York. The breach formed at the site of a partial channel that cut into the barrier island from Shinnecock Bay.

Five months after the storm the Works Progress Administration constructed a 1470-foot long bulkhead along the west side of the inlet. The eastern edge was not initially reinforced, but by the mid-1950s jetties were completed at both the east and west sides of the channel, stabilizing it at 800 feet wide in a north-south orientation. It previously flowed at a north-east / south-west angle.

Sand accumulated from longshore drift has filled in the beach to the end of the eastern jetty, while the beach beyond the western jetty is prone to erosion and is periodically mechanically replenished by USACE. The Corps also maintains the 0.7-mile channel's ten-foot depth and 200-foot width, which leads to an inner channel six feet deep and 100 feet wide that provides access to the Long Island Intracoastal Waterway. In the last two dredge maintenance projects for Shinnecock Inlet, 302,000 cubic yards of sand were extracted in 2004 and 500,000 cubic yards of sand were extracted in 2010.

Shinnecock Inlet, ocean side, facing east
photo: Nestor Rivera Jr.

Shinnecock Inlet

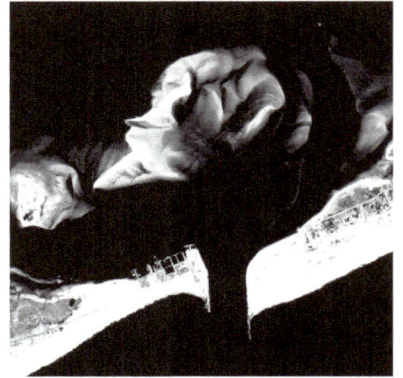

April 1994

November 2006

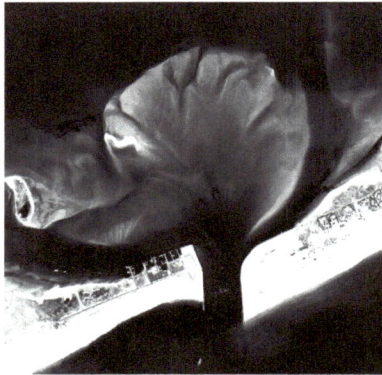

March 2007

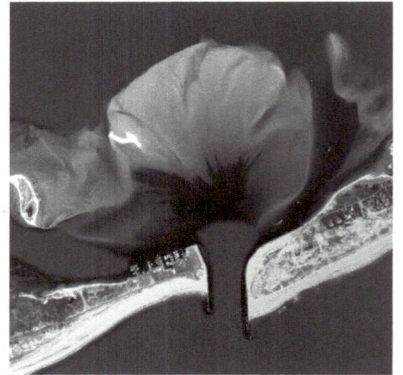

October 2008

September 2010

November 2011

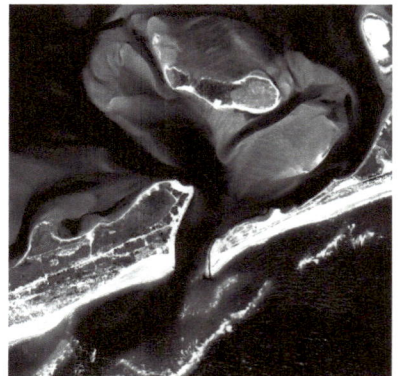

March 2012

April 2001

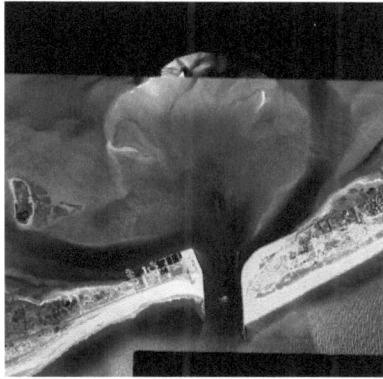

April 2004

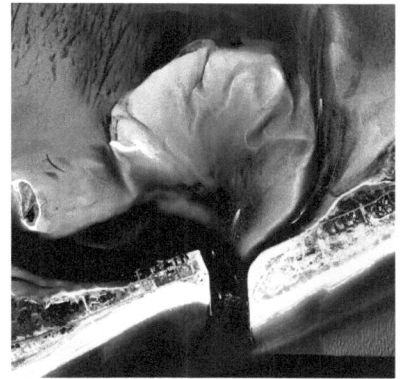

October 2006

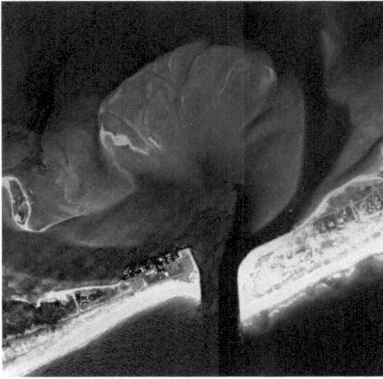

September 2009

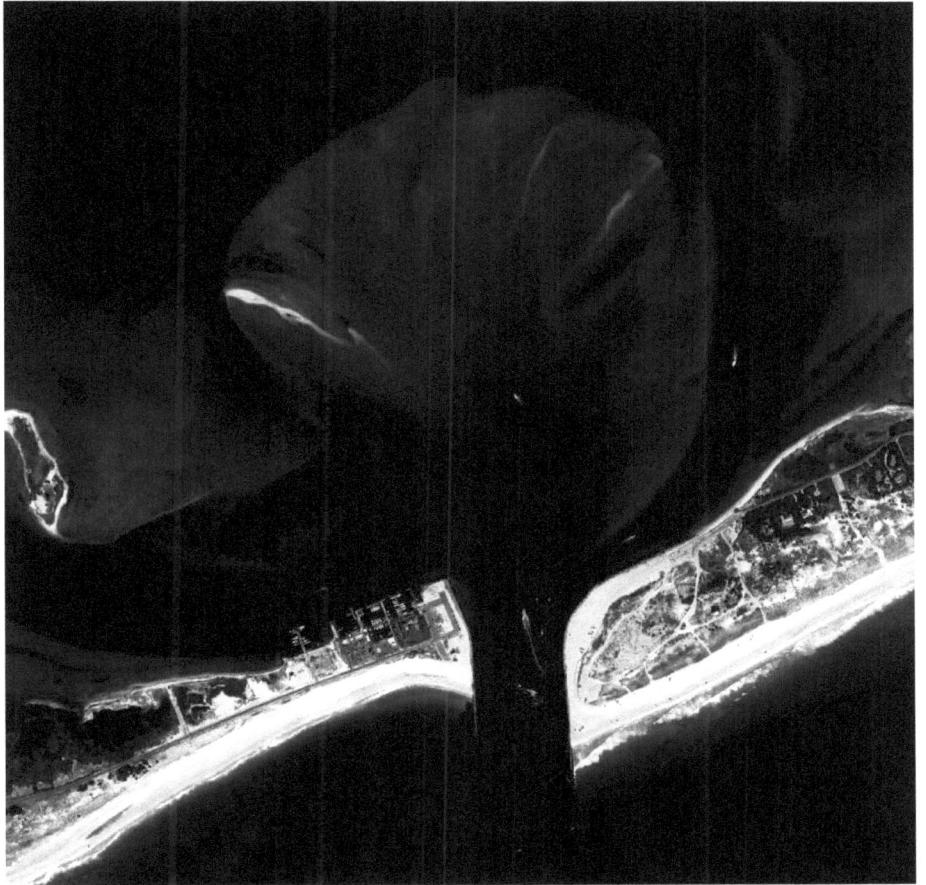

November 2012

September 2013

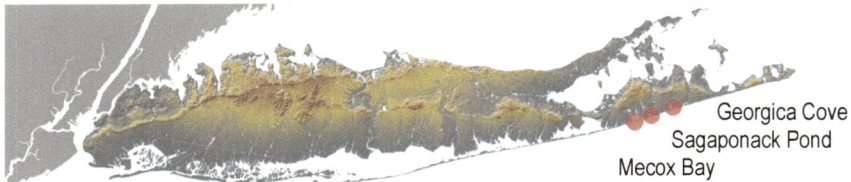

Georgica Cove
Sagaponack Pond
Mecox Bay

Breach at Mecox Bay, looking north, May 2009
photo: USGS

Mecox Bay, Sagaponack Pond, and Georgica Cove are artificially breached, generally annually, to alleviate flooding when water levels threaten the surrounding neighborhoods. The breaches close themselves through littoral drift. Mecox Bay was also breached during Hurricane Sandy in October of 2012 and mechanically closed.

Georgica Cove is a 290-acre coastal lagoon separated from the Atlantic Ocean by a 330-foot sand bar. The cove is managed by the East Hampton Trustees who control a cycle of mechanical breaching where a channel is dug connecting the lagoon to the ocean, draining it of fresh water and replenishing it with ocean water. This is performed to alleviate flooding when the water levels in the lagoon threaten surrounding properties and also as a way of regulating salinity for habitat purposes. The breach then typically closes naturally through littoral drift. For example, in April of 2008 the cove's water level was nearly five feet higher than the ocean, and a 20-foot wide channel was dug that expanded to a width of 150 feet through the force of the outflowing water. The water level in the lagoon fell, salinity increased, and the breach closed itself in five days.

Breach at Mecox Bay on Long Island, looking north, November 2012
photo: USGS

Breach Cut at Sagaponack Pond on Long Island, looking north, March 2005
photo: US Army Corps of Engineers

Georgica Cove, looking east
photo: HipHamptons.com

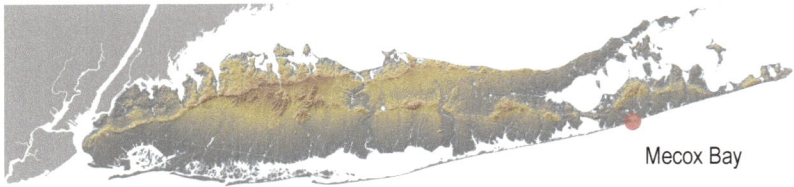

Mecox Bay

April 1994

October 2006

November 2006

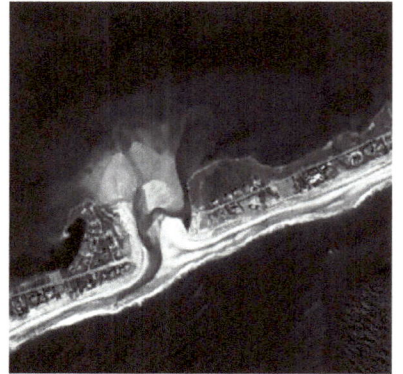

March 2007

September 2009

November 2011

March 2012

1998
photo: US Army Corps of Engineers

April 2001

September 2006

October 2008

November 2012

September 2013

Sagaponack Pond

April 1994

November 2006

March 2007

October 2008

September 2010

November 2011

March 2012

April 2001

September 2006

October 2006

September 2009

November 2012

September 2013

Georgica Cove

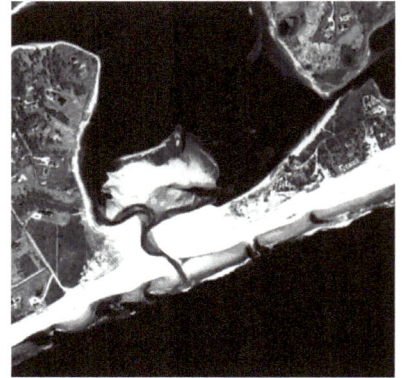

April 1994

April 2004

June 2006

17 September 2006

May 2009

September 2010

May 2011

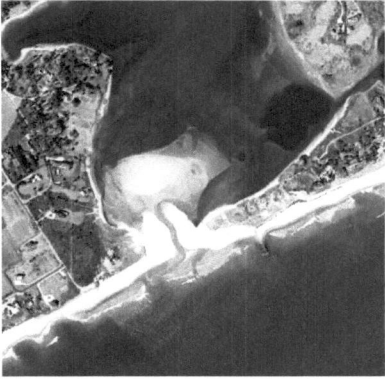

March 2001

30 September 2006

February 2007

March 2012

November 2012

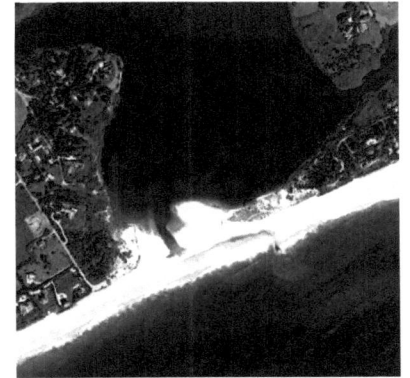

September 2013

West Pond Breach
Jamaica Bay Wildlife Refuge

West Pond, Jamaica Bay, looking north, 1994
photo: Don Riepe

East and West Ponds, two freshwater ponds created at Jamaica Bay Wildlife Refuge in the 1950s under the initiative of the Parks Commisioner Robert Moses, were breached in October 2012 during Hurricane Sandy. As rare fresh-water sources in the area, the two ponds draw a great diversity of species to the heart of the Jamaica Bay Wildlife Refuge. Their maintenance and accessibility are considered integral to the Refuge's educational and recreational value.

East Pond breached from within and was immediately restored given its proximity to the A train subway line. The Draft General Management Plan for Gateway National Recreation Area leaves the West Pond Breach open while restoration and management options are explored. Although the pond was artificially constructed, and in fact was somewhat brackish before the breach, many advocate that the breach be filled and the pond's fresh water habitat restored.

Another option is to leave the breach open, increasing the opportunity for valuable salt marsh habitat, and to either stabilize it or allow it to evolve. Breaches through barrier islands often close themselves over time as littoral drift brings sediment along the shore and eventually fills the gap. This is unlikely for West Pond, however, where there is very little fresh sediment introduced into the back bay system. The force of tidal flow and future storm events could in fact increase the width of the breach.

A compromise position put forth by the New York City Audubon Society restores approximately half of the original pond to fresh water and allows the rest to remain tidal salt marsh. This plan also prioritizes public access, ensuring the continued value of the Refuge as an educational and recreational resource.

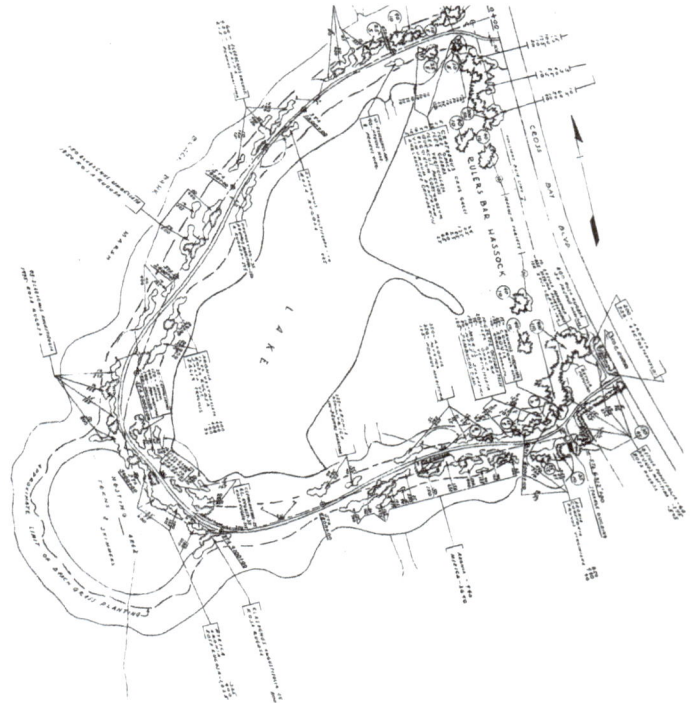

Plan for West Pond, Jamaica Bay Wildlife Refuge, 1954
source: Courtesy of the City of New York Department of Parks and Recreation, Map File

Breach at West Pond, Jamaica Bay, looking east, June 2014
photo: © Vertigo Aerial Photography for SCR Jamaica Bay

West Pond Trail, September 2013
photo: Kjirsten Alexander

November 2012
source: Google Earth

NYC Audubon West Pond Concept Plan, 2013
source: SCAPE / LANDSCAPE ARCHITECTURE PLLC

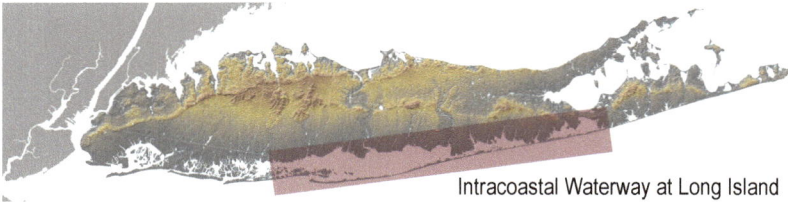

Intracoastal Waterway at Long Island

The Intracoastal Waterway (ICW) is a 3,000-mile navigational channel that runs parallel to the Atlantic and Gulf coasts behind sheltering landforms. Much of the ICW follows natural inlets, bays, and sounds, while certain stretches are manmade canals. In 1807 Treasury Secretary Albert Gallatin wrote that the waterway would allow travel "secure from storms and enemies." It was intended not only to facilitate commercial activity, but following the War of 1812 it was also considered an important national defense strategy. Today the ICW is largely used by recreational boaters and some commercial barges, as well as the US Coast Guard.

The 1824 General Survey Act made the US Army Corps of Engineers responsible for improvements to and maintenance of navigational waterways. The Rivers and Harbors Act of 1937 authorized the Long Island Intracoastal Waterway Navigational Project, a total of 33.6 miles leading through the Great South Bay, Bellport Bay, Narrow Bay, Moriches Bay, Quantuck Bay, and Shinnecock Bay, then north through the Shinnecock Canal to the Peconic Bay. Sand from maintenance dredging of the six-foot deep, 100-foot wide channel is locally placed on the oceanside shoreline for beach and berm replenishment and habitat restoration.

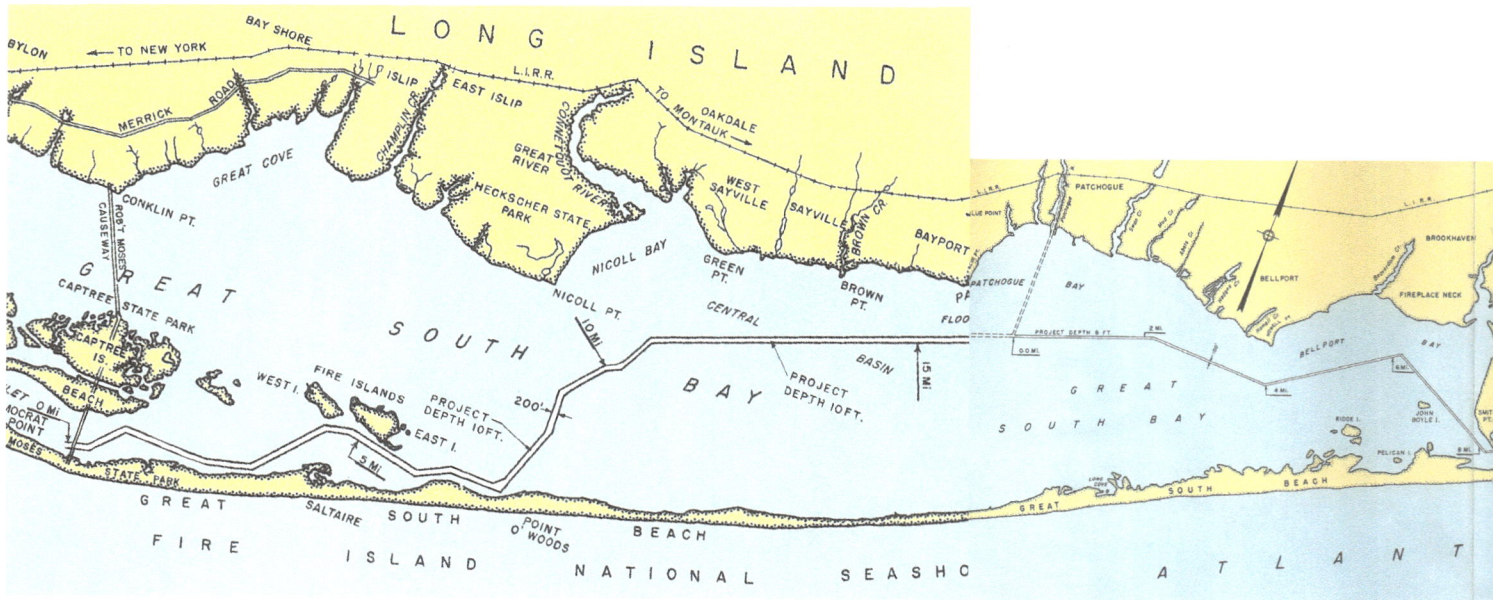

Long Island Intracoastal Waterway Channel
source: US Army Corps of Engineers Project Maps Rivers and Harbors, Maps 22 and 24, 1986

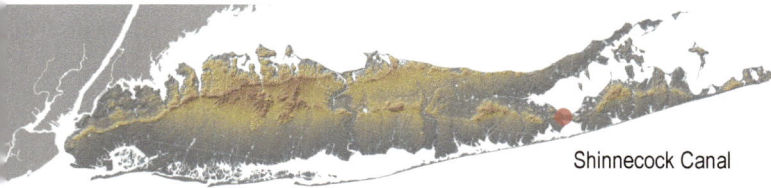

Shinnecock Canal

In 1892, construction of the Shinnecock Canal was completed through the South Fork of Long Island, connecting the Great Peconic Bay on the north side to the Shinnecock Bay, Long Island Intracoastal Waterway, and Atlantic Ocean on the south side. The canal is 0.9 miles long and 100 to 180 feet wide.

A lock system was completed in 1919 to protect the canal from the currents and erosion resulting from differences in water levels between the Peconic Bay and the Shinnecock Bay, which have opposing tidal cycles. The lock system includes three passive tidal gates which are pushed open by the northern flow of the incoming Shinnecock flood tide and the outgoing Peconic ebb tide, and pushed closed when the flow reverses. Hydraulic locks 41 feet wide and 250 feet long allow boats to navigate the up to three-foot vertical difference when these passive gates are closed.

September 2013
source: Google Earth

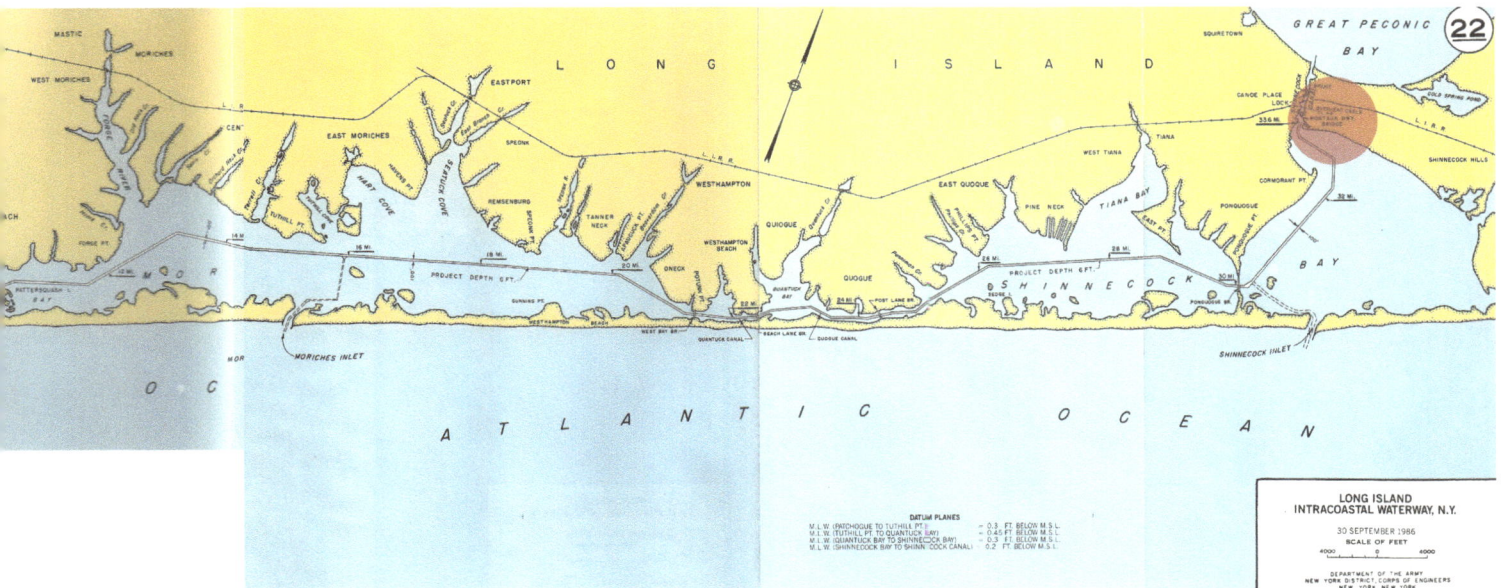

LONG ISLAND
INTRACOASTAL WATERWAY, N.Y.

30 SEPTEMBER 1986
SCALE OF FEET

DEPARTMENT OF THE ARMY
NEW YORK DISTRICT, CORPS OF ENGINEERS
NEW YORK, NEW YORK

Saw Mill River, Yonkers

Beginning in the 1920s, USACE subverted the last half-mile of the Saw Mill River into an underground culvert from "Chicken Island" to its conflux with the Hudson River. In 2010 the City of Yonkers began to daylight six blocks of this long-buried stretch of river. The first phase daylights a two block section that passes below Getty's Square, and eventually six blocks in total will be revealed. The project creates 13,775 square feet of aquatic habitat and includes features that enable the American Eel to migrate upstream. The new channel flows parallel to the underground tunnel which now acts as an overflow pipe to protect the surrounding urban area from flooding.

source: http://www.sawmillrivercoalition.org

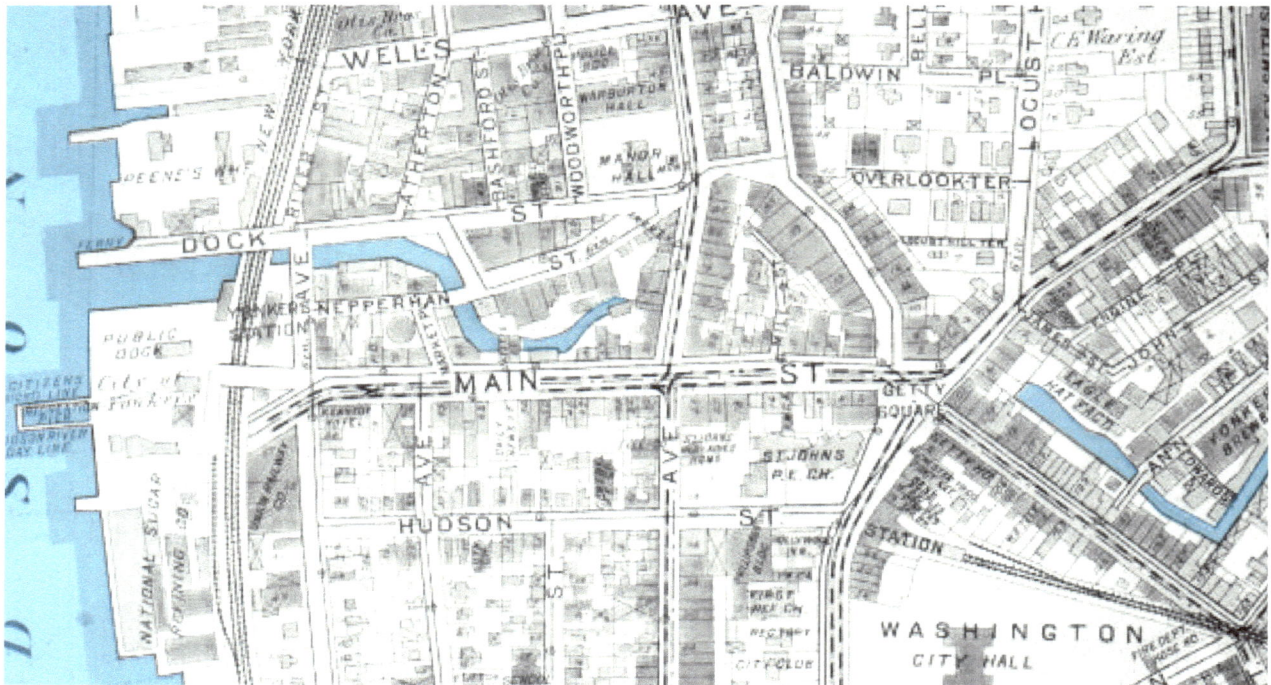

Map of Yonkers showing Saw Mill River partially covered, c. early 1900s
base map source: http://www.sawmillrivercoalition.org

2010 (prior to daylighting)

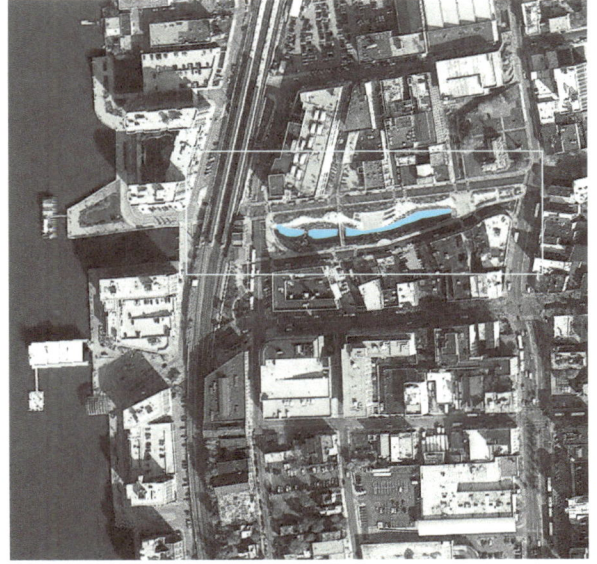

2012

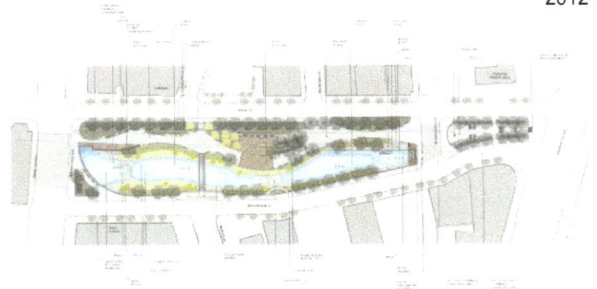

source: DaylightYonkers.com

photo: Steve Duncan / Waterfront Alliance

source: DaylightYonkers.com

Gowanus Flushing Tunnel

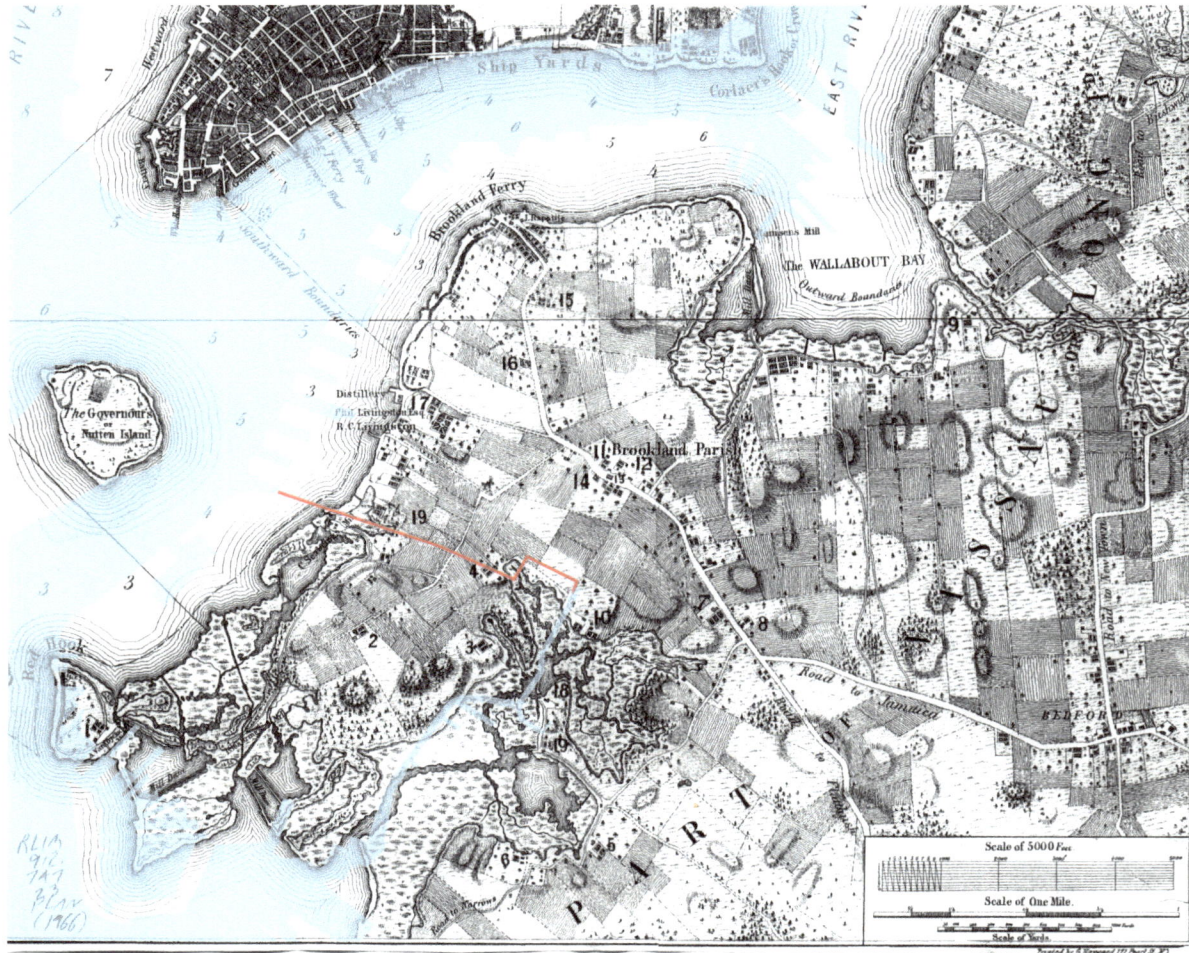

Map of Brooklyn, 1766, with existing waterways (blue) and approximate underground path of Gowanus Flushing Tunnel (red)
base map source: Wikimedia commons (public domain)

Terminus of Gowanus Canal, c. early 1900s
source: New York City Department of Environmental Protection

Renovating the Gowanus Flushing Tunnel, 2011 (original brick work remains intact)
photo: Fred R. Conrad, The New York Times

Constructed between 1905 and 1911, the Gowanus Flushing Tunnel operated for nearly half a century, pulling water from the Gowanus Canal below 1.2 miles of Brooklyn streets to the currents of Buttermilk Channel and the New York Harbor. Having stood mostly idle since the mid-1960s, the pumping station with its 12-foot diameter flushing tunnel underwent a full renovation from 2009 to 2014 and is now functioning once again. With three new submersible pumps, the tunnel can carry up to 252 million gallons of relatively clean, oxygenated water per day, now in the reverse direction from Buttermilk Channel to the Gowanus Canal.

Edgemere Overwash Plain and Flushing Tunnels
Floyd Bennett Tidal Marsh Inlet
Fort Tilden and Jacob Riis Overwash Plains

Proposed Flow at Jamaica Bay

During Hurricane Sandy, the protective dunes on the ocean side served communities on the Rockaway Peninsula well—they were neither overtopped nor breached. However many of the homes along the peninsula were flooded from the bay. Flood waters accumulated and had only one outlet to retreat: Rockaway Inlet at the far western side of the bay. Even after surging ocean waters retreated, it took time for water to drain out of the inlet, prolonging the flooding of the Rockaway Peninsula and back bay communities.

Given this history of back-door flooding as well as the high residence time of waters in Jamaica Bay (an average of 33 days), this project explores the possibility of planned "overwash plains" at key points along the Rockaway Peninsula to allow for periodic water and sediment exchange. This exchange could improve water quality and provide a vital sediment source for marsh island accretion, as well as provide outlets for the retreat of surge waters within the bay. The overwash plains are strategically placed in areas with existing low-lying topography, in some instances where channels used to exist, and where there is minimal interference with existing development and infrastructure.

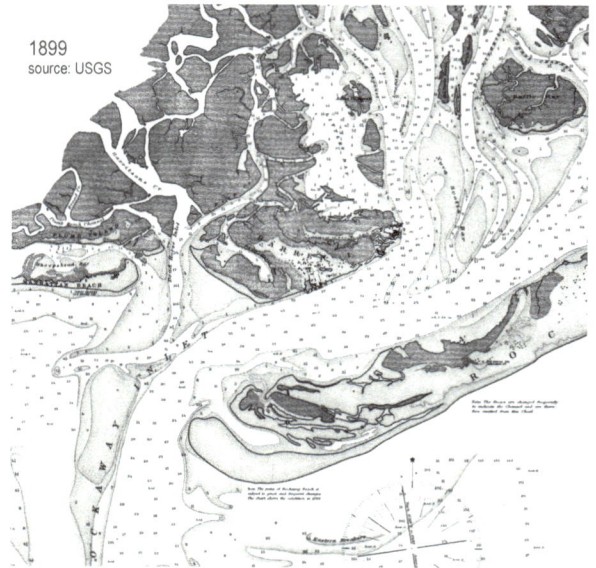

1899
source: USGS

A tidal marsh inlet behind Floyd Bennett Field adds marsh acreage and increases circulation from Rockaway Inlet to Mill Basin. Overwash plains through low points at Fort Tilden and Jacob Riis Park encourage flood waters in storm events to cross the peninsula between, rather than through, the communities of Breezy Point, Roxbury, and Neponsit.

1899
source: USGS

JAMAICA BAY

At Edgemere, the least developed and lowest lying areas with partial inlets at Norton Basin (Beach 35th through Beach 33rd streets) and Little Bay (Beach 49th Street) are reconfigured as planned overwash plains that flood in distinct stages. Additionally, subterranean flushing tunnels allow continual water exchange between the ocean and the bay, improving water quality in areas of the back bay with the deepest borrow pits and highest residence time.

In a 1964 US Army Corps of Engineers report, a navigational inlet was proposed from Norton Basin to the Atlantic Ocean (above, top). 1897 property drawings from the Town of Hempstead Municipal Archives (above) show the former Norton's Creek, which used to exist at this same location. This creek could be recreated as a navigable canal, or its former path could be defined as a simple depression to serve as an overwash plain.

www.ingramcontent.com/pod-product-compliance
Lightning Source LLC
Chambersburg PA
CBHW060826270326
41931CB00002B/79